La Plata Cantata

La Plata Cantata

Poems by Jim Barnes

Purdue University Press
West Lafayette, Indiana

Published 1989

Library of Congress Cataloging-in-Publication Data

Barnes, Jim
    La Plata Cantata : poems / by Jim Barnes.
        p. cm.
    ISBN 0-911198-96-2
    I. Title.
    PS3552.A67395L3 1989
    811'.54—dc 19   88-17071
                                                                  CIP

Printed in the United States of America

For the memory of my mother and father,
Bessie Vernon Adams Barnes and Austin Oscar Barnes

CONTENTS

ACKNOWLEDGMENTS

Many thanks are due Northeast Missouri State University for a generous grant in the summer of 1987 which allowed me to cast this book in its final form. Many thanks are also due Neil Myers, professor of English at Purdue University, who made several helpful suggestions. In addition, grateful acknowledgment is made to the following publications in which many of the poems, some in slightly different versions, first appeared:

Amelia: "Learning Balance"; *Bamboo Ridge:* "Night Letter to the Secretary of the Interior"; *The Bloomsbury Review:* "Below the Sans Bois Mountain" and "Paraglyphs," except the first section; *Boundary 2:* "Dreams the Children Had"; *The Chariton Review:* "Trying to Read the Glyphs"; *Cincinnati Poetry Review:* "The Game"; *Confrontation:* "Behind the Lumberyard" and "Urn Burial"; *Denver Quarterly:* "Great Plains Tornado"; *The First Skin Around Me: Contemporary American Tribal Poetry:* "The Submarine in the Park Between the Muskogee Toll Road and the Arkansas River"; *Green River Review:* "Surveying Near Ellsworth, Kansas," under the title "Two Poems on One Theme"; *Hayden's Ferry Review:* "Going After the Milch Cow" and "Souvenirs"; *Interstate:* "Stations," under the title "Pumps"; *Kansas Quarterly:* "Ubi Sunt "; *Kenyon Review :* "Bandstand" and "Santa Fe Depot, Sundown"; *The Laurel Review:* "Crossing the Kiamichis Again," "For the Suicide," and "The War Over Holson Valley"; *Long Pond Review:* "At 39: The View from Sycamore Tower"; *The Missouri Review:* "Gill Netting the Beaver Pond"; *The Nation:* "Domain"; *New Collage:* "In Hugo Country"; *New Letters:* "Circus Poster," "Icons," "Memories of Oceanside," and "Once in Winnemucca"; *Nimrod:* "Postcard from Blue Finger Lake"; *Ohio Review:* "Turkey Season"; *Paintbrush:* "Heavy Metal," "The Light Above the Store," "The Palace Cafe," and "Savage Country"; *The Phoenix:* "Near

Cimarron, New Mexico"; *Poem:* "The Heavener Runes," under the title "Rune"; *Poetry Northwest:* "Touching the Rattlesnake"; *Poetry Wales:* "The Pastor's Farewell"; *Quarterly West:* "Bombardier"; *River Styx:* "Deer Camp: Blue Mountain"; *Sulphur River:* The first section of "Paraglyphs," under the title "Petroglyphs"; *West Coast Poetry Review:* "Something in the Blood"; *Winewood Journal:* "South Williamette Valley Bars: A Memoir"; and *Zone 3:* "Hunting Winding Stair Mountain."

The poems "Trying to Read the Glyphs," "Domain," and "The Submarine in the Park Between the Muskogee Toll Road and the Arkansas River" also appear in a limited edition volume, *The Fish on Poteau Mountain* (Cedar Creek Press, 1980), copyright 1980 by Jim Barnes.

GILL NETTING THE BEAVER POND

1. PACKING

Strange to think after so many years
that I worried about what to take
fishing overnight up Holson Creek.
It seemed I was leaving on a journey
I had my doubts about. But an odd
sadness made me see the washed out
road leading through the hills without

the many ruts and rocks. I did not
know how deep a night was. I took
too little food and a quilt I would
not use. I remember that I thought
of storm, of being taken under
by some monster in deep water
while we defied rain and thunder

to stretch our net through the shadows
of trees on the pond. I did not pack
one fear intentionally: I acted
the twelve-year-old I surely was,
hoisted the duffel up on my
back, and marched to cadence like
a good scout should before he dies.

2. THE NETTING

We had heard stories of big bass,
lunkers wallowing like grown hogs
in the old beaver pond near the bog
where cottonmouths parted the grass
at night. My brother knew his way
in woods and water and I stayed
close on his heels at the end of day

after we had set the gill net.
The sun had fallen red into
the timberline, and the pond grew
immense before the lingering heat
turned chill. The quiet flap of bream
we thought tangled in the net seemed
a portent of a bounteous stream.

At midnight we ran the net. No
bass, no bream, but half a dozen
eels squirming, crying their human
cries, and their soft round faces so
full of pain I could not hold them
in my weak sand-coated hands. A dim
moon rose. We skinned and gutted them.

I knew I could not eat their flesh,
but morning woke a hunger in
my head, and I ate what I had been
in the deep night in a dream of fish
when I had hung limp, by the gills,
tangled in a web of threads no eel
could mistake for Sargasso swells.

3. DRIVING HOME

No matter where I looked the low
mountains were waves on some blue sea
I'd lost my way in. At my feet,
on the floorboard in a wet toe-
sack, six other eels lay in the slime
of their only defense. Low limbs
clutched at the windshield as we climbed

up the rutted road that led home.
The motor made a steady whir,
and I thought of cold spinning stars,
for a reason I cannot fathom,
unless my mind had taken on
some migrant trait not everyone
would want to trouble with. The sun

somehow was still setting as red
as the evening before, and the high
thin stars began to offer light
webs across the sky as we reached
home. I felt myself suddenly caught
at twelve by a motion I could not
stop: I swam in the night like a moth.

Surveying Near Ellsworth, Kansas

All that's left is hard,
the bone-dry creek,
the knife shade of a single tree,
the prairie burned brown by a screaming summer sun,
and a lone marker,
stone, belonging god-knows-where:
scalped 1853.

THE HEAVENER RUNES

Old words vague
as reeds on water.

Gouged runes
cold as glaciers.

Who can tell
a thought
from stone?
Only the glyph
speaks.
Thought is lost.

The thing itself
remains.

Hot earth.
Cold sky.
You between.

To make a mark
you become the mark.
Your name.
A woman's.
The date.

It does not matter:
you are the mark,
you are the stone.

NEAR CIMARRON, NEW MEXICO

The wind you can never face,
heavy enough to bruise an eagle's back,
whips cactus bare as bone.
The only sundown that you can believe
in is a lone horseman
racing across the plain
toward everything that he owns
and nothing that is his.

GREAT PLAINS TORNADO

Thirty miles away
it stands still,
a pillar of sky,
dark with the antiquity
of Roman coins,
shattered mosaics.
Byzantine.

Fluted stone,
joints of lead
somewhere always
crash and fall
on a prairie acropolis
and strew for states
artifacts hammered
to useless seed.

SOUTH WILLIAMETTE VALLEY BARS: A MEMOIR

GOSHEN

Many an exile
has done time
in the Goshen Bar,
suspended
between home
and the promised land.

EUGENE

The Oasis
stands just off
the main drag,
home for confirmed drunks
and would-be sheiks of Araby.
Here hot air is constant
in the liquid Oregon night.

The Sahara Club,
its sands run out,
hides behind a new facade,
the genteel Eugene Carriage Trade,
dress code rigidly upheld. Once
you didn't have to drop your jeans
to enter here.

SPRINGFIELD

The Driftwood
catches the dregs
of the mighty Mackenzie
and drunks who were only always
passing through.

CRESWELL

The Roundup—
rocking rider
and broken neon lariat—
longs for the good old days
when honest drunks
knew how to dance, how to ride
the voluptuous woman
behind the bar.

COTTAGE GROVE

The Dog House,
pointers and *setters* at the rear,
is sanctuary for hunters and loggers
and two lovers gunned forever down.
The wallpaper: buckshot and blood,
the pride of Cottage Grove.

CIRCUS POSTER

With lion couchant
below
and tiger couchant
above

the blue rainbow
spells
your eyes,

arches over
rearing horse and whipping
rider,

her tights
wondrous
O,

and two clowns
all mouths
sighing

the white air
that fills
the ballooned words.

ONCE IN WINNEMUCCA

Eating soggy bean sprouts
in Winnemucca, Nevada, at dusk
after a hard day's drive
was poor tribute to the opium tin
I'd kicked out of Jakeleg's mine.

Stringy things, fried by a red-haired Swede
who said he herded sheep in winter.
My rockhound summer was ending under
the blue light of plastic lanterns.
Through the wall I heard a jackpot ring.

I wondered how a Chinaman felt
in Winnemucca's snows and what the tin
had in common with a sweating Swede.

The lanterns "made in Ft. Smith, Ark."
gave off an opiated glow.
I hitched my sagging Levi Strausses
about my hips and left the frying
Swede without a tip.

STATIONS

Texaco
(trust
your
car)
reeks
(to
a star)
to high
heaven

Shell
(sans
s)
connotes
sea

Deep Rock
promises
(a
cool
death)

Phillips 66 (6)
(power
to
give
life
unto
the
image
of
the
beast)

Flying A
(ultimate
re-
ward)

12

Dreams the Children Had

The fall the circus did not come
was gloom only the children understand.
The weather was mad: the owls went
screaming through the trees, and some

lone dog was always barking on
a leash. Nights elephants traipsed
the sky, their trumpets sounding depths
of the children's dreams, and Bongo

the midget grew a giant, his stilts
booting across oceanic beds,
and now and then a muffled dread
swelled the waves in the children's quilts.

But the children slept, and less aware
of world: their clouds rolled, billowed into
a spangled tent of night and through
symmetrical rings of mind and air.

The children's eyes grew perfect, round
in sleep. They sang to the calliope,
danced the perfect rings, and then the
dangerous beasts laid themselves down

even at the children's feet. The first
fear they may have ever had was gone.
This was their world, their true home,
and stars splayed down upon the earth.

ICONS

FOR SAM RAY

1. HAND

Imprint of a hand.
On the stone
when the stone
was soft. The perfect
hand of a child,
the lifeline clear.
A hand outside time.
You see but do not see.
Take this hand.
The aura around the tips
of the fingers stays.
Here. Forever. Where
there was a hand
a hand still is.
Hand beyond a hand.
Meaning beyond meaning.
Meaning.

2. GAPS

The birdmen. Some
would say thunderbirds.
Only the glyphs speak.
There is no thunder.
The mind bends to seize
the stone. The image
is unchanging. The mind
closes too many gaps.
Open. The gaps
must stay open.
The birdmen hold
the stone. There
is a force I cannot
name. This force on
and in the stone.
Obviously, I cannot
even name the stone.

3. ICONS

Time does not exist
except as a corridor
through which I pass.
There is no going back.
But the speed at which
I proceed is not constant.
Nor is the speed with which
I perceive. Moments in
the mind need icons
to identify the contours
of space. There is more
to be learned of the past
than will ever meet the eye.
I have forgotten more
than I will ever know.

4. NAPE

Sight has weight,
substance, is matter.
Lucretius early knew.
Consider the back
of my neck. I will
turn to greet you
eye to eye.
Friend.

5. ROOM

Images of the past
dwell in each house.
Foundations.
I need a room
of my own so that
I can meet myself
every time I return.

6. TONIGHT SOMEWHERE

For the first time
I see Venus balanced
on the sharp horn
of the scythic moon.
Not star within the
nether tip, but star
at swordpoint. There
are wars we have
forgotten. My god!
for the first time.
Tonight somewhere
on a vast desert
a pillar of fire
will amaze small
creatures, and they
will wait on elbows
for nothing
like understanding.

SOMETHING IN THE BLOOD

Blue Mountain. I know it
by the pines: knotty green
and sick on turpentine.
Deer camps fill thin air
with the smell of gutted does.

A return after months
of mountains of other sorts
to find a drunken ranger
squatting by the spring.
His right. And mine to drink:
the iron-cold water hones my blood.

This is home: we all come back
to kill. Something in the blood.
The bucks know and head due north
to the Fourche Maline, water
still stinking of Frenchmen
somebody's forebears killed.

I check the action of the 30-30,
slide hand-primed cartridges home.
A fox squirrel leaps limb to limb,
eying the elk-horn sights.
The finger tenses, eases off.
It's something in the blood.

Trying to Read the Glyphs

A hundred feet straight up this cliff's dead face
some hand chiseled glyphs. Abstract and open
to every sundown. To read these riddled runes
I have to chew the wind from caves I can
never know. Somehow the glyphs are right, in
this cold stone no glacier has ever kissed.
I expect a foothold, a niche to level on,
a ledge some wild lover knew before the leap,
but find only stone vertical as split ice.

A thousand years dead, the waterfall pours
dry fire into my eyes. The acid of
my sweat grooves the painted face fingers
claw into. The eyes reject my touch as I
pull the glyph to me like a departing lover.
I am body for the etched face I cannot
read. Flesh and stone, my mind is full of bones
the caves hide in webs thick as arctic snow.

Below, the river that I long for now
inches past, like a glacier hunting for
the sea. The shadow of a lone hawk spins.
Images of what I love fall with the sun,
and night brings me down, both shoulders sore
with bones I never knew I was heir to.

POSTCARD FROM BLUE FINGER LAKE

At a cove on Blue Finger Lake I pitched camp,
hurrying to get the explorer up
before the promised shower soaked me through.

My wife's pale face kept haunting canvas corners:
she had not smiled at my weekend madness,
but had shaken her head, whispered something vague.

The rain beat down on the flapping tent, then stopped,
which was also promised. I looked over
the lake's water being pelted, far out;

and then I breathed a somewhat purer air.
Dear wife (I envisioned a postcard showing what
she'd missed), would you believe there was a rain-

bow over the tent? I miss you. No, I don't.

Touching the Rattlesnake

The neighbor's leg was black from toe to thigh,
with yellow pus oozing from cuts he'd made
trying to stop the poison from reaching
his heart. He showed the three of us stumbling
into his house, after Sunday school set
us free, what he said we would be afraid
to see. The swollen blackness made me shudder
with adolescent sins I knew we were doomed
to hell for. He dared us to touch the leg.

Tight as the shell of a dried gourd, the skin
seemed to break with each slight movement he made.
I left with the smell of venom in my lungs,
my eyes careful with every rock we passed
on the way to the swimming hole. I lay
on the shoal and felt the current crawl along
my body until all thoughts of fangs were washed
away and the rattle of leaves above my head
seemed only leaves. *Amazing grace, how sweet*

I sang straight up into the Sunday sky.
The others splashed my face, and we wallowed
like carp in the mud. We could not know that one
of us would die before the sun went down, fangs
buried in his neck as he reached over a boulder
to pull himself up the face of the cliff above
the swimming hole. Nor that he would live just
long enough to climb back down, boasting that
he touched the snake before it struck his neck.

The neighbor did not die, but thrived on guts
he said it took to have a snaky leg.
I could not forget the oozing blackness
and never crossed his door again, nor how
white the naked body of my friend lay.
The wind rose late that day and made the limbs
crash above our heads. That night it rained.
The sound of thunder and shotguns carried us
through a domain of snakes we would annihilate.

HUNTING WINDING STAIR MOUNTAIN

The sky overcast, a threat of thunder
murmuring up the heavy south kept us
from hearing the trailing hound until the rush
of wind our way told that he had treed more

than we had set out to find on that day.
The forest of oaks and knotty pines obscured
even more the hazed sun we thought we had
a bearing on. I knew the dog would die

if the three coons decided he was no
real threat. With one shot my father took
the smallest one. Climbing, the others shook
with rage across the canopy of low

pines. I know we did not hunt for the sport
of it. I long ago forgave my father
for whatever sin it was that I swore
we were being punished for when we heard

the lightning strike the tree the dog still barked
up. The silence that followed filling the woods
I can't remember feeling since. We could
not find our way under the impending dark

that kept us from keeping the mountain at
our backs. The rain pelted us with some fierce
determination. We did not know north
from south, east from west, up from down, nor that

night was yet hours away. When the sky did
lift, the mountain loomed upon us like the storm.
We had not known it lay so close to home
that we could be halfway up the darker side

waiting for the moon or sun to take us down.
The old dog smelled of burning sulphur all
the way down the steep slopes on our slow heels,
his eyes surprised still by the god of coons.

FIRST CAVALRY:
HOLSON VALLEY ROAD, 1942

The column passed on a slow Sunday—
cannons, half-tracks, and silent men
olive-green in the valley sun.
Before the dust of its passing

had settled I saddled the roan
and holding a gallop followed tracks
as far as daylight still allowed.
Dusk fell like a dare a long way

from the bivouac. I did not turn
back until I heard the mountain
lion. I reined the roan into
a full retreat: his flanks were foam

before we reached the barnyard gate.
Loser of a lesser war, I felt
my hair bristle at the wild cat's cry
and then my father's stern "Dismount!"

THE WAR OVER HOLSON VALLEY

Across the moutain somewhere lay Texas,
where all the warplanes were migrating to.
Day after day they crossed the valley low
and humped to miss Winding Stair that blocked
the southern sky. You knew nothing of radar
then, nor that Texas from Dangerfield to
El Paso was a vast training ground for
Air Force personnel.

              The valley knew the war
mainly from the thunder of heavy bombers,
the silver engines of fighters echoing on.
Forty years and you remember clearly
the P-38's twin fuselages barely above
the trees behind the barn, the slow milk cows
bellowing into stampede, their milk turning
bitter as gall. The radio gave you news
of the theatres of war, and you wondered
about the language of it all.

                  And now it
roars back, the innocence you were guilty of,
the guilt for years of playing war with friends,
who later left the slow valley for the quick
world, their Purple Hearts boxed among other
souvenirs. You knew it wrong to like the war,
its mystery of leathered men and wild machines.
Still, you imitated flight, with whittled planes
in the canopy of oaks and pines on the slopes
of Winding Stair. Wind took your hair by night,
and you crashed in fierce resolve, waiting
for morning's resurrection in pure air.

Bombardier

1.   Bathing in Lethe

He came back broader, taller, than I had
remembered, his duffel full of wonders
he gave to me: compass, model B-17,
medals, ribbons, and silver wings. What's more
he made his aviator's cap fit my head.

For two green months that short summer we fished
the mountain creek across the open fields
our father plowed throughout the war. The bass
we caught he insisted we throw back, to
keep the stream alive he said. I wondered

why we walked the banks to try the deep pools
or shoals and why at dusk each day he stripped
and bathed so reverently in the spring-fed
stream while I thrashed about, torpedoing
a convoy of minnows or a frog. Now

I see I missed the mark. We bathed at home
with regularity. But the stream was
more than bath, more than an instrument
of cleanliness. The water sang a way
to be; the wind on ripples mapped our lives

with contours we couldn't see. Then my brother
was gone. The daily drone of planes from Tinker
Field told me he was gone again to war,
though in my mind I knew him bathing still
in a cool stream that washed most worry away.

2. SOUVENIRS

A hundred pictures of the London Blitz
or more he sent back, the postcards a pale
sepia and held together with Red Cross
gauze. When he wrote, the V-letter came crushed
by many hands, through many lands. Once
even it bore a postmark from Morocco

and a stamp from Roma. We never knew where
he was nor how. He sent an Iron Cross
from a base somewhere near Brussels in '45.
Just before the end, he sent me another
B-17 someone had whittled out
of Black Forest pine, its metal props

snipped out of a prewar tobacco can.
My mother loved the Irish linen. My
sisters gasped at the wonders that he sent
them, little things that made the marvelous
seem true. We placed the souvenirs along
the mantel and window sills and read his words

about a wider world he was going to help
us see. The war filled us with dread, so too
the age into which we grew. It was his way
to give us hope, the souvenirs, mementos
of being there, wherever it may have been
before he disappeared over the Netherlands.

3. MIA

The letters did not stop, and packages
periodically arrived for months after
the telegram. We knew the mail was slow,
but with fixed minds we saw him alive still
somewhere over there above the clouds bound
for places he would send us pieces of.

And then all stopped, and we began to think
of death camps that, before, we doubted ever
were, of how he might have glided in—to
crash into the walls to make a gate through which
the suffering could flee or simply to just be
there passing out mementos of the world.

No word ever came that he was found, nor
has it come. Forty-odd years and still I
feel him in the air, hear the sputter of
dying props that do not die, but whir on
into the dreams I have of this my life
that is also his life. Somewhere along

the lines of blood, it must be clearly written
we will not forget to honor the poetry
that daily then shaped those lives: the lost children
of the holocaust singing through open flames,
the welcome home for those who stood it all,
the bombardier still on his one last run.

4. THREADS

Through the maze of years, I have stumbled on
too many tokens strewn about like bones
and have seen too little of the world I
think he meant to light. In the receding
sounds of planes flying far above his lost

domain, it is not just my fading brother
I sense the loss of. Something else drums
into the void, something once so big I
knew it would never end. I'd like the past
always flooding back: a river, a sea,

a soothing mist of atmosphere. I thought
I would remember roads we walked, the way
back after the setting out, the open doors.
Artifacts I hoped were private now belong
to others. I see them in the houses of

strangers, or gutted in windows of pawnshops,
their bright mystery tarnished by hard hands
that cast them away to live. Somewhere there
must be threads to piece together, threads
leading back to that simple complex time.

THE SUBMARINE IN THE PARK
BETWEEN THE MUSKOGEE TOLL ROAD
AND THE ARKANSAS RIVER

Gunmetal gray and salt with years
the submarine strains
toward the toll.

I never stop in all that passing.
Nobody does. Flags
on the conning tower

all always the same:
storm and squall.
But the wind's

a constant cheat.
Deadlocked belly deep
in red sand,

the boat is prey
to birds and Air Guard trainer jets.
Across the 4-lane,

half a world away,
the bartender knows
the North Atlantic

a pool of icy puke,
a lone Indian speaks
in an unknown tongue,

and two whores remember the war
they wore flags in
and swear

they'll blow this town
when the sky wakes up red
and their ship comes in.

Memories of Oceanside

The dark jetty
and one dead shark, mouth gone white
against the sea.
A flood of images
incoherent as the California sun
and you are back 30 years,
pollution, that biblical word, not
reinvented yet, in wide screen.

The boardwalk
and a few small honest booths.
You shot arrows at balloons,
an innocence at noon,
after your first long swim
in languid waves, the tar balls
a mystery of the deep.

Nights
of knives and bad dreams.
Appendix out, right flank scarred
and netted tight with dissolving gut,
you dreamed your fame
came applauded by the squawk of gulls,
a forethought no vision could quite hold.

Anchors
into this inland sea.
Here in these late times
you know only
sharks plastic and fulltoothed
above the waning pinball machines,
your good ghosts ebbing
slowly, slowly, like all sand,
down into the hollow night
where the fool is silent
and the clown forgets his nose.

THE GAME

The mad dog barked because he had to bark
at the dangerous shadows leaping toward his eyes:
we pulled his chain and clamored up the oak

in a fine delicious fear of teeth as sharp
as the spikes of stars spinning atop the trees.
The mad dog barked because he had to bark

at threats he defined as cruelty at the throat.
Oh, those were the nights we could win any prize:
we pulled his chain and clamored up the oak,

his nose objecting to our heels, his joke
not quite the same as our own, but surely close.
The mad dog barked because he had to bark

and play the game his captors chose, but spoke
his words his way, a merry rage set loose:
we pulled his chain and clamored up the oak.

We loved that fierce beast and the deadly stroke
his paws gave our dogged legs and skinned knees.
The mad dog barked because he had to bark:
we pulled his chain and clamored up the oak.

Ubi Sunt

Things were larger then and vaster,
full of wonder that would register.
When you go back again for good
to where you best remember you stood—
amazing and true, the philosophers'
sight! Frogs, weeds, and gophers'
holes, you seldom even notice.
How small, now, the wild oat is.
There's a shrinkage that overcomes,
vanishes ants and clover bums,
deflates skies, stunts trees, fences,
and generally assassinates our senses.
O, but we must wash the whole world
in explanational blather and swirl
all essence that is not pure or plain
right down the heady sewer main,
or else the dirt piles high again
and mountains grow and comes the wind
whipped by ravens' wings and magic
rules as once we knew it did. Tragic
that education makes us bigger,
moves finger from nose to hair trigger.

NIGHT LETTER
TO THE SECRETARY
OF THE INTERIOR

In brown silence
the cheat grass falls
to its light task
below Spirit Mountain.
A spreading brown
is taking the hills,
and the mountain
will drop its green
before the salmon
make one last run.
Here at the center
of our last world,
we try to tell you
it is wrong to take
away the trees, to
let the cheat grass
claim the sinking
hills and stones
tumble from their
source. A smothering
earth cannot breathe
without the hair
of branches and eagles
in unbending wind.
Spirit Mountain
we will hold
when all else

is broken by your
will and odd way
of suicide. Only
a few now we
are growing daily.
Soon we will stand
before you like
a forest of legs
to trample your
floors as soft as
the virgin earth
was before you
sent the yellow
Cats and screaming
saws and dishonest
drunks, whose eyes,
white putrid flesh,
we stared down
Saturdays in town.
You will know us
though it will
be too late
for parley or
compromise. We
were seduced
to make us late
in moving from
ancestral perches.
But we have moved.
Beware.
Expect us soon.

Domain

The hawk sweeps in on a wing of the sun,
breaks to a stop, trembling and still,
like a skater at the perilous edge of ice
breathing a silent strength. Until

he places me in his domain
there is no movement of wind, talons
as rigid as old pitch around
the branch, the eyes steady as stone.

Then, only then, does he fall
into sundown, his eyes pointed
as swords, into the stand of spruce,
into some lair, through its dark heart,

down the hollow of the windfall night.

Day on day I walk these woods
and never hear a sound. Then from
nowhere: the terrible beating of wings,
the panicked cry, the toppling home.

This domain I walk carefully in,
aware of the eyes that pierce, the hand
that fells. It is not my place to
speak, nor the place where I began,

and I will not take from the hawk
the beating wing, from the prey the one
last cry, the sun its wing of light.
Only: I count my fears here, down,

down the hollow of the windfall night.

PARAGLYPHS

Two fish,
definitely carp,
picassoed in stone:
Holiday, Missouri.
In certain light,
flesh scales
under lichen.
Hot stones hiss
into the water pot.
There is a song
to the night moon
and to fish.
This cave, this mouth.
There are echoes
still.

•

This arc of moon, this scythe,
burnt by the light of eyes
into savannah sandstone.
What's lost concerns me
more than what may be.
A collector of old nests.
This arc of moon, this scythe.
Overhead a hawk, a shining.

•

The red ochre snake
may be seen in two lights.
A snake, horizontal, long,
sunning, recumbent.
The life of a man, the valleys,
the peaks, the slopes
and rising of the eyes.
And one other: enemy of heels,
brother of bonds,
the vein of life
I flow into and through.

•

I am a survivor of the sea
I do not understand.
Even the turtle,
that intrepid wanderer,
is better equipped than I,
a road map on his back.

•

On the banks of Holson Creek,
a short half mile from where
it joins the Fourche Maline
in silent flow to wind
farther east to the Poteau,
I found on the surface
of the rutted earth, after
a hard spring rain, 3 finely
worked arrowheads, 1 rough
spearhead, 1 broken adze,
2 pieces of thin clay pot,
and 1 large fragment of
a human shinbone. I call
this spot the Place of Acorns.
The white oaks along the banks
of the rivers bear fruit
the size of your fist.
A wholesome food, pure
protein, when leached.

•

Flying over Big Sur,
I think of Miller.
Houses hanging in
ravines, lovers
copulating in doorways.
The civilizing gray
and heavy air. All
tropics are rooted here.
Manifest destiny rainbowed
in radical dream,
and nowhere to go.

•

Cuzco:
the hitching place of the sun.
The sun stood still
on anchored and fitted stones.
And the earth stood still
in its socket of sky.

THREE SONGS FROM
A TEXAS OILFIELD

The cardinal drills
the brilliant dawn,
his cry as sharp
as a diamond edge.

•

The jay does not call
thief! thief!
Cousin to the crow,
he objects to darkness:
this bright land is his:
fief! fief!

•

In pecking order
the flicker is king
of ground and trunk:
dressed in black tie
and hammered yellow vest,
he speaks with the authority
of a pile driver.

AT 39: THE VIEW
FROM SYCAMORE TOWER

To climb this shaky thing I came
too many miles and from a woman
I could have been drinking bourbon
with. The view is blue for forty
miles every direction except
west, where Buffalo Mountain humps
hard against the sun, its tower
making this one a derelict.
Map and triangulator long gone,
the lookout's table is runestone
for adolescent loves and relics
of the master race. The valley hard
below and north is now scrub oak
or sparse pine where I stepped barefoot
on my first rattlesnake, and saw
a naked neighbor chasing heifers
through the woods. I knew his life was
running out his deaf ears and he
out of himself. I knew fear for
dead days and could not look him full
in the face on Sundays when he led
the valley's only choir. The river
is blue as sky, the way it touches
nearly every house, then snakes
along a field and hides in trees
beyond the ridge. Running water
and running lives from this distance
are hardly more than blue ripples
in wind. The air is rare, chock-full
of ghosts and insects, and home
is always ten thousand miles away.

BELOW THE SANS BOIS MOUNTAIN

The buck had come down the draw in silence,
so quietly that in my stand I did
not know he stood in shadows of the pines
until the sun began to break the edge

of the mountain into splinters of light.
Then I saw him from my perch on the rocks
just above his head. My camera was not right
to catch him in any kind of decent shot.

Two hours before the false dawn I had dragged
my sleep-filled body up the mountainside
and set my lens toward where the mountain sagged,
waiting in half-sleep for the midsummer sky

to open on the rim. His eyes were fixed
toward the Sans Bois as if he, too, would take
something of the sun if it were given. Sticks,
stones, the broken ridges began to fade

into the light they were made of. The solstice
opened in ribbons of sky and cloud, a bourn
I would record on film, while the buck licked dust
and rubbed the bloody velvet from his horns.

In Hugo Country

A snowbound Crow smokes
beside a stove fired red with pitch
and counts white buffalo
cracking on the barroom wall.

The sky is sharp at 20 below;
the landscape always backed
by a mountain you never want to climb.
You learn the Flathead on your right
drove piles in Venezuela. Or stormed Iwo.

Sometimes you predict the weather
wrong and never hear a song for months.
You've got to be around a while
to know the land is real
and how to love under a ton of blankets
when the stove turns back to blue.

Horsefly, B. C.

Tired of climbing schist
and hard heights
of honey trees,
the last bear moved
to Banff for kicks
and Hershey Bars.

Tourists think it odd
that anyone could love
and die in Horsefly, B. C.,
and with their chisels
break away the names.

Those fading houses
flanked by scree
say welcome
to any soul or wind
the mountains send
to Horsefly, B. C.,

Once there was a man
from Horsefly, B. C.,
came down to Calgary
for the Stampede,
never went back—
think of it—ever
to Horsefly, B. C.

CROSSING THE KIAMICHIS AGAIN

Each trip in time becomes the same.
It's hard to remember separately.
I am driving across again.
The mailboxes have aged.
But still I see your name,
by the stone where it should be.
Now in this full dawn,
sentences of light strike the road,
and I read what I can
before the dance of heat
erases your good words
and the shouldering pines
grow dark under the raucous crows.
Day is breaking this time,
and I am still driving for Texas
and another sky I'll never find.

La Plata Cantata

1.   Turkey Season

In early morning light you see them rise
from the branches, give their feathers a shake,
and drop gently down to the ground, their cries

scraping through the woods to herald daybreak.
You must hold still, black as the trunks around
you: no movement at all, nor eyelid tick.

In all the stalks the absolute you've found
is just this: not stealth, savvy, camouflage,
but your mind's immersion in the will of dawn.

These birds you hunt know more than swale and ridge
or weather rising fierce in the sudden south.
On days when your luck runs along the ledge

in easy shot, you count the lives in both
light and dark, the sum total of your frames.
What you take away from these woods and off

the land is spirit you hold in trust. Names
of birds and beasts erupting like wild dill
upon your tongue say that you did not tame

one wild thing, nor cause the low sky to spill
its rose or blue. Your camera holds a way
to be, and you another through your will.

2.   THE PALACE CAFE

We sit here with our backs to the wall and drink
to all the things we should have done before
Armageddon fell upon this town. We think

we know it well, the mountainous cloud that bore
the very soul away, its winds whipping
roofs away, walls. It took the wives we swore

to God we'd love forever, honor, and sing
the seasons to. And took our sons. And then
our farms. There was total nothing on the wing

but cloud and wind. If we are lucky when
the waitress comes, coffee in hand, she might
say a word that will take our minds up wind

from this stinking town, what's left of it.
But we do not know it well: the changing sky
does not allow forecast. The winds that hit

us in the back that day filled the blank eyes
on the square with debris. The Palace lost
its shade, the window and a rack of pies

gone without a trace. The tornado cost
the Sabre Jet a wing, the park its trees
and tulips that survived the last hard frost.

With all the loss you'd think we'd want to leave
the state. We stay with nothing like we want,
save The Palace where we don't have to serve.

3.   BANDSTAND

When I was just a boy, I crawled down
from my Red Flyer and under the old
bandstand, which was warping even then round

the edges of the floor. You could not know
what wind and wonder had moved to that dark.
I tell you there were mysteries that now

seem stranger still than all I knew to stalk
my nights. The bandstand was hideout for Huck
and Tom, pure heaven for the local pack

of budding musicians, den for dogs. No luck
is what we had: killer bees established hives,
they said. Now look at this stone block that took

an hour to pour, a bandstand with no give
underfoot, and underneath—no love. They
sold the old one to Hutterites. I believe

it's now a floor to a communal barn, hay
hiding lost bad notes and my honeyed sin
written on dark joists. So the sidemen play

and the leader sways on crumbling concrete in
all the festival we have. I say here
it's not the same: we need the darkling wind

beneath to lift the music from the fear
of remaining horns. From this stone kiosk
we cannot know the music of our sphere,

cannot know the beauty of arabesques
graved in wood, nor the tap of heels beneath
trombone and flute, nor the darker humming risk.

4.   THE WATER TOWER

Below the *Class of 86* fading
whitely above the winded catwalk boards,
two lovers strain to hear the same old song

they have heard radioed each night before,
since the song began and they, as lovers,
chose the moon as anthem. Under the water

tower, the light of the low moon covers
the song, stills the whispering voices that hold
the wind at bay, stills doers and movers

even in the town at large. The lovers fold
into themselves satisfied with the night
under the water tower, where the bold

hand has written its destiny in light
script and fading paint. Stark against the out-
lined sky, the tower claims its stilted right

to be the fountainhead of love and doubt,
billboard of fame, sentinel of a jerk-
water town, four-legged moon long gone out.

5.   THE SANTA FE DEPOT

The sun sinks into the westering tracks where
they come together in a thin steel line.
The sky turns molten and consumes the earth

at the low line of trees where fields begin.
Another day, another day, the old
reverberating phrase tolls against a wind

that rattles bones in this low place and folds
the past in a book you can't read. *Another day,*
the farmer's words for what he does not hold,

and for what he does. To stand here and wait
for the westbound train, you'd think the depot
had a life beyond the little lives that date

the hill: hues of sundown begin to flow,
and the cracked walls take fire. Shadows and lines
mark the station's empty seats. What you know

now means less than what this moment is in time:
another day, another day you have stood
here or anywhere to be counted in time.

6. BEHIND THE LUMBERYARD

We used to slip into the lumberyard
at noon to smoke before the stack of two-
by-fours caught fire and they put up a barbed

wire fence six strands above our heads to do
what nothing else had done. We eyed the fence
and shied back into jimson weeds and blue-

grass gone to seed among the larks and wrens.
Before the big storm took the lumber piles
up into the blinding dark, I told my friends

I'd bet they'd never find us here, not while
the school year lasted. Our science teacher
did, plastic sack in hand and an odd smile

across his face, later, one day after
school. He stuffed the bag of long thin leaves
into a pocket and broke into laughter

we could not see a reason for. Toward the
end of summer he was gone. By that day
we all were hooked on Lucky Strikes but free

from the oozy knowledge that he could say
something to our folks we knew well to hide
or lose so much it'd take our breath away.

7.   THE LIGHT ABOVE THE STORE

The grocer never blew out the light upstairs
until his wife committed suicide.
Why he let it burn when kerosene was scarce

no one could say, though I knew she was mad
before the English had left Picardy.
Sometimes through the window I saw her clad

only in a gossamer gown, herself ghostly
in the soft lamplight, from where I stood below
those few nights during that last liberty

after Pearl. When I came back from Iwo
less a man, the shrapnel wounds were slow to heal,
and she was madder still, the sickness so

severe she danced naked across the field
beyond the water tower before her man
covered her with a ragged quilt he held,

running, like a flag. I was there again
below the window when she screamed *oh God,
take me,* and nothing came except the rain

that forced me in. The night she took the drug,
he left. I was there a silent witness,
my eyes blurring against the coming fog.

Time was never right for that peculiar loss.
Nights, still, I think I see her there, wavering,
outlined by a globed flame in the gathering frost.

8. SAVAGE COUNTRY

No one stands seven feet tall in La Plata,
not since Dent (alias Robeson) wrote
the Man of Bronze into the pulps, the data

wrong but Doc Savage right in a world not
to be ignored. Gone by 1959
Dent and Savage had saved their world from rot

and this town for posterity. But dime
magazines shelved forever under glass
can't keep the park alive, nor bring back fame

once it's faded through death's door as it has
here, where nobody knows Doc's name. The band
in the park is seldom musical. No mass

of blooms on the sad square will ever stand
over anything for long. The growing season
is short so far north, and the city hands

no longer serve the finer arts, the reason
given always the same: winter potholes
must first be filled and work on streets begun.

The town has grown as practical as moles:
all movement is toward greater things that sate
the sense of hunger of lesser human souls

than Savage and his cohorts had. The fate
of this Missouri town is wreathed on our
front doors, and what we know we learn too late.

9. Heavy Metal

My sign is Cancer, but that can never mean
I have to live under an ordinance
that would shut my mouth till the water's clean.

I don't think we should leave our health to chance,
not when our cancer death-rate is so high.
I told you when I ran I'd take this stance:

to admit our mistakes and rectify
the sin of heavy silence held too long.
We need to stop this useless talk and try

to set things right: admit the report's not wrong,
close the city lake, forbid the sale of
fish. The presence of heavy metal has hung

about us in the mist rising from the bog
each night and in the crawling things at water's
edge. All the children that have died, their dogs,

the cattle—let us say that something matters
more than the festival and tourist buck.
We've got to call the experts now to gather

samples once more of everything from shuck
to fin. Our grave mistakes are resting on
the hill. Let our stony silence have struck

its last blow. This has not been a good town
to believe in. Perhaps it will toward the end
when we can say we did all that could be done.

10. URN BURIAL

When the elevator blew its top and fire-
balls shot a hundred feet into the air,
no one expected much of a loss. The gyre

of smoke was blacker than should have appeared,
though there was but little concern. Firemen
contained the blaze at noon, the 4-H fair

hardly delayed two hours, the parade in
progress before the church bells chimed at one.
The wheat was totally destroyed within

the larger bin, and the soybeans had gone
bad because of water damage. Insurance
made the owner smile at his telephone.

But then the sad thought came. Across the fence
the Chief had stretched to keep the children safe,
the wind stirred a mound of wheat. The chance

that anything could have been alive may have
caused us to count heads: one hired hand now lost.
We clambered up the remaining walls to save

our honor in sight of God and the First
National Bank. We knew him dead. Of course,
he'd caused the fire by lighting up. The burst

of light that caught his final act to force
him into what must have seemed a tall sea
of grain is one a simple oiler of doors

and dust fans could not know even if he
did survive, which he did not. We disinterred
his seared and suffocated form, while the

remaining walls circled us like an absurd
urn we could never dig out of, not in
this town even with the help of our lord.

11. The Annual Soybean Festival

It's the same old song we heard this time last year
when the lead guitar got sick and couldn't hide
it behind the mayor's daughter in her

coronation gown. The music always slides
from swing to rock as the day wears down resolve:
so hard it is to keep our notions tied

when the dark creeps in and our children dissolve
into motions we were always afraid
to make, whose forms we now stand in awe of.

This festival designed to celebrate
the bean and buck has gone too far astray:
Mennonites and Maconites, Iowegians of late,

Kansas Citians and Columbians pay
to grace our fairground with aluminum
cans and assorted cast-off crap. We say

each summer we'll stop the sale of condoms
and light beer inside the city limits,
but never make it law. We kept the bums,

however, well at bay: we gave no permits
for camping down by the tracks when the hobo king
suggested we coordinate times and sites,

put our festival and their conference thing
in one bin, as if to suggest the cost
were slight. They went on to Iowa, having

no other choice, long before the first frost.
Our crops grow smaller every year. We plant
and harvest with the almanac. Thus boast

we know what our fathers did, but we can't
seem to make our shrinking dollars equal
our bad debts. No matter how we may rant

and rave, one thing is sure: this festival
will stand as long as there are beans and banks.
Of what we've done, indeed it's best of all.

12.   THE PASTOR'S FAREWELL

FOR J. H.

To live here is to know the threat of storm
well enough to say it is no big deal
soybeans don't grow and our fields are foreign

landscapes to the eye. We tried too long to seal
our fates in silos packed with grain, to say
oh God, we're rich to the deliberating squeal

of sons we never knew would rule the day
the way we ruled the soil we took to till.
Friends, we are coming to a time we lay

our burdens on the closet shelf with will
and testament and want to go out clean,
and in that landscape of desire we fill

a grange hall with light laughter and, in
the center ring, the children we forever
want to be, all threat of storm within

our lives denied. Now the lovers' long star
burns out, now the river finds another shore,
now we become, now we end with what we are.

For the Suicide

The moon glides on water, the surface
black ice no one could walk on long
enough to count a heartbeat. Full,
dull moon that a gnat's eye could dim
or a lover's sigh could cause to slip
too soon into its darker sleep.

No one knows you are here, a risk
dared and done, your hands clean as stone
tumbled on the beach two hundred feet
below. Not one night bird cries, not
one wave sounds. The dark that touches
you consoles: your eyes write your name

on the offing you cannot see, nor
wish to see. You stand at the edge
of things—this cliff, tomorrow, your
life—and all the while not one song
for you to understand. To look
into the dark, you risk it all

and forever fail. Something triggers
need, and lovers fall. The ship sails
on, always toward the sunlit land.
The millionaire knocks on other doors.
You have no home inside your skin
that opens when the heart tides turn.

DEER CAMP: BLUE MOUNTAIN

At the western edge of the last ridge, you
wonder why the mountain stopped and refused
to turn the stream. The rutted road down ends
in the river bed. You make your camp in shadows
you no longer recognize. The way the water
charms you into yourself remains a mystery
constant as the sun. This was your larger
home when you were small. Now nothing is yours,
not even the deer, plentiful as ticks.

Two miles away the house you were born in
continues to buckle under the relentless
skies, though it never seems to lean toward
the river behind the barn. Sundown and you
hear ghosts of old dogs bark, two miles away
and ten thousand in curved time. The only
bridge across the river has recently
collapsed. The fences you remember have
disappeared into a forest of heavy pines.

You know why you came back, but cannot find
the words to put the wind right with this world,
the one world you had and lost. You're the kind
of fool that lets the deer browse in his camp.
Thank God for that. The only shot you'll take
is with a 35mm, and then only if the light
falls right. Those forty years seem a long shot.
From this angle of repose, you think it's
worth a try—to frame another kind of life.

From the Swinging Bridge

The shadows of bluegills seem
rapid arrows of light against
the vague algae and stones.

Swaying above the river
takes more breath than
good swimmers have to give.

Breathless in the rocking air,
you see your time flow
in the dark water
that will not stay
for shadows on the swinging bridge
nor ripples on the plane of sky
twenty feet below.

This parallel time behind
the deep water you look into
makes you want to step down
from the middle
and sink softly into
a dim semblance of self
that lives quite other.

But you cannot step
out of the swinging arc
of wind and your will
until the motion dies.

You walk across the water,
not into the dimmer sky below,
and feel the bridge
lift you upward with each step.

Photo by Carolyn Barnes

Jim Barnes is author of *A Season of Loss, The American Book of the Dead, The Fish on Poteau Mountain,* and *This Crazy Land.* In 1980, Columbia University awarded him a translation prize for *Summons and Sign: Poems by Dagmar Nick.* Barnes is editor of *The Chariton Review* and professor of comparative literature at Northeast Missouri State University.

More poetry from Purdue

FISHING WITH BLOOD
Fleda Brown Jackson
"A splendid collection of poems with the special merit of being both intensely artful and equally interesting. No one to my knowledge has written better about Georgia O'Keeffe, and many have tried. Fleda Brown Jackson has a good wit, a sharp eye, and a tough character."—Dave Smith
96 pages, ISBN 0-911198-94-6, $6.50

THE SPINE
Michael Spence
". . . a strong, clear collection. Its spare imagery is absolutely appropriate for the human and natural landscapes it evokes with both economy and grace."—Joseph Bruchac
76 pages, illustrated, ISBN 0-911198-89-X, $5.75

A SEASON OF LOSS
Jim Barnes
"[He] moves with assurance from the past to the present, linking them firmly in his vision and helping his readers be authentic in thought and feeling."—William Stafford
80 pages, illustrated, ISBN 0-911198-75-X, $5.50

THE ARTIST AND THE CROW
Dan Stryk
"A reader finds landscapes or settings, and their inhabitants, that come alive in richly textured but unvaryingly precise language."—Ralph J. Mills, Jr.
96 pages, illustrated ISBN 0-911198-71-7, $5.25

ALL THAT, SO SIMPLE
Neil Myers
"[He] writes with such artistry that whatever he presents us with appears in its essence."—Arturo Vivante
72 pages, illustrated, ISBN 0-911198-56-3, $4.00

41   48